I Bought a Pearl

I Bought a Pearl

NAOMI M. WONG

Copyright © 2024 Naomi M. Wong. All rights reserved. No part of this book may be reproduced in whole or in part by any electronic or mechanical means without written permission from the author, except in the case of fair use as defined by Section 107 of the Copyright Act of 1976.

PAPERBACK ISBN: 978-1-7377275-5-2
EBOOK ISBN: 978-1-7377275-6-9

Cover art by: Mirza Yasir https://www.fiverr.com/creative1artist

Published by Naomi M. Wong

naomimwong.com

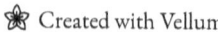 Created with Vellum

From pearl to pearl
From love to love
From me to you

Introduction

> *"Again, the kingdom of heaven is like a merchant seeking beautiful pearls, who, when he had found one pearl of great price, went and sold all that he had and bought it."*
>
> — MATTHEW 13:45-46 (NKJV)

The Parable of the Pearl is a beautiful illustration of costly love. There are differing interpretations of what exactly the parable is highlighting about the kingdom of heaven. If we understand the merchant to represent God, then the pearl represents the entire cosmos (inclusive of, but not limited to, humanity), which God redeems at the cost of God's own self—a very great price, indeed. Another view could cast as the merchant any Christian, who upon seeing the incomparable value of a life in Christ, gives up all worldly desires and goods to pursue it. While I find both interpretations helpful in different ways, this book will mainly reflect on the latter.

At the time of this book's publication, I will have been committed to Jesus for twenty-seven years, following him intentionally for fifteen of those. I can wholeheartedly say that the decision to follow Jesus was the best—and, as I make it every day, it *is* the best—of my life. What God gives to me through the person of Jesus Christ has saved my life in many ways. My relationship with Jesus has been my most precious possession through times of rejoicing and times of sorrow. And the longer I live in this relationship, the more I come to understand that the cost of obtaining it was not just a one-time, upfront payment. Sure, I said a sinner's prayer when I was five years old. But selling all that I have for this relationship has been a lifelong process—often a painful one. The cost is real, though worth it.

I Bought a Pearl is a collection of modern-day psalms through which I seek to portray glimpses of the incomparable value—and some of the cost—of following Jesus as well as the struggle to make sense of it all. I speak to God in a raw, honest voice to show that we can invite God into every aspect of our lives. The poems in this book express a desire to please God, even in struggles associated with embodiment, waiting on God, and interaction with other Christians. I often engage with biblical texts, imagining myself in biblical scenes or commenting on the characters in them. So, I hope that knowing this will encourage you to engage this text, and the biblical ones, critically.

DEPENDENCE

With respect to my life in Christ, dependence upon God is the departure point and the destination and the road under my feet. That is why the first section of this book will reflect on dependence in depth. Most Christians are aware of the need for God, at least intellectually. If we believe that God is the almighty creator, we understand that we need God in order to exist. However, ask a room full of Christians how precisely they depend on God in their daily life and you may be faced with blank stares.

I have been painfully aware of my need for God since my early twenties. At that time, forgotten childhood traumas began to resurface in my mind. I became extremely disoriented and struggled with ordinary processes like emotional regulation. At the time, I did not have access to the kind of mental healthcare that I would have needed, but God intervened.

I want to be clear that I am very much a proponent of therapy when it is available. That said, I also believe that God heals however and whenever God chooses to heal. In my case, God stepped into my mental health journey, bringing life-giving truth and irresistible, steadfast love that began to heal me. Of course, my healing was not instantaneous. It has been a journey with God very much active and at the center. Daily, and from moment to moment, I interact with God through prayer in order to function and to thrive.

I composed the poems in "Dependence" during a season of Lenten reflection. That year, rather than fasting from food or social media, I chose to commit to writing a poem on the same theme (dependence) once per day. What emerged was a touching snapshot of my relationship with God, in which God is portrayed as a loving and attentive caregiver. It is my joy to share these poems at the beginning of the book because they emphasize what I believe to be the heart of our faith: God with us.

For sure, Christian faith should be expressed through loving and justice-oriented action. But beneath the things that we do is who we are, and above all else, we are loved by someone who will never stop loving us and longs to heal and help us, if we would allow it. To live from this place of dependence keeps us grounded and fuels our love and our justice-seeking. God's love is life. That makes some of the less enjoyable aspects of life in Christ—the mystery of unanswered prayer and the painful moments of living among God's people—not just bearable but worth it.

COST

This section is different from the first and the last in tone as well as content. The similarity is that it does primarily contain prayers. However, it also includes some poems that are not prayers, and the subject matter pertains to wounds inflicted by the church. There are many costs—social, political, spiritual, and physical—to following Christ, so my treatment mainly of church wounding represents a very narrow sliver of the cost of discipleship. I have chosen to focus in this way because this kind of cost is often overlooked.

"Cost" holds in tension the reality of deep wounding caused by the church and a desire to remain faithful to God. The poems in this section make a statement collectively, and therefore, no one poem is meant to stand in isolation. Think of a psalm like Psalm 137 that, when taken on its own, is a snapshot of pain that only tells a portion of a story. The greater story is richer, and far more redemptive, than one would guess at the end of that psalm. The same is true of many of my poems, and it would be best to remember this when reading "Cost".

The tone of this section can be wild and full of rage, at points: emotionality that is rarely welcome coming from a woman in the church, and especially the daughter of two vocational ministers. In a sense, this section of the book is the love letter most children of Christian ministers did not know that it could be appropriate to write.

While the content in this section gives voice to great pain, it is not merely an expression of emotion. I am no stranger to the rage of justice-seeking Absalom or the bewilderment of nearly-sacrificed Isaac, but "Cost" is a *plea* for God to enter these pain-filled emotional places. Ever read the Book of Job? I live by the truth I find there: that at our invitation, God makes God's presence known, and hope and healing become possible.

I have no desire to plumb the depths of the specific situations that led to my wounding. They are simultaneously particular to me and relevant to many. It suffices to say that I have experienced the church as a place where gossip, insincerity, lust, sexism, abuse of power, and racism run rampant. This is particularly unsettling given that members of the church are meant to love each other and the world the way that Christ does.

Since my young adulthood, it has been my conviction that I cannot fully have Christ without his Body, the church. How this fact has grieved me, at times! But I cannot overlook it. Christ is the Lover of My

Soul, and I *must* have him. And to have him, I must be a part of his Body. So, I remain committed to it. And, most mercifully and lovingly, he remains with me.

As for the hurtful and harmful actions of the church, I find no life in excusing them. I do, however, trust in God's almighty ability to heal the wounds that we as a community inflict upon each other and the world. From my own experience of God as healer, I know that the most painful wounds are not inaccessible to God. Perhaps God allows the imperfect community to remain, to help in the ways that it helps and to hurt in the ways that it hurts, exactly because God is able to save us from ourselves and from each other.

FAITH

I chose to end the book with this section because faith, the value of it and the pursuit of it, has been both a central factor in my relationship with Christ and a never-ending source of questions for me. The poems from "Faith" were composed during another of my Lenten reflection times. The result was interesting, since this season coincided with a season of disappointment and waiting.

As you will see, I found that faith and doubt were more deeply linked than I had previously believed. My roots in evangelical charismatic spaces had not prepared me for that outcome. At one point, I realized that I actually had no idea what faith was, despite having attempted to cultivate it for most of my life. And I further learned that, while I choose to have faith—however that may be defined—it is very good news that God's faithfulness is greater than my own.

I Bought a Pearl is about the intermingling of the preciousness of a life in Christ with its costs. There will be plenty to digest. I pray that your journey across these pages will be a life-giving one in which you are encouraged to invite God into your own experiences, wounds, sorrows, and joys.

The following section is a prayer that I wrote at the beginning of the season in which I composed many of the poems in this collection. I believe it is a fitting transition into the rest of the book as it contains all the elements of the following chapters: complete dependence on God, the cost of life in Christ, and issues of faith. May you perceive God's presence in my journey, and in yours, as you read this book.

NO MORE SONG

I have no more song, though lots of love pent up. My sweetest Love, forgive my silence. I am less bitter than choked with pain, devoid of breath. I was in shock years ago. But somewhere along the way, shock gave way to nothing.

It is not nothing; I am sad. But this is a sadness unlike any I've had. Other times, I knew there would be an end, no matter how distant. But I've experienced too much of your church to believe that I will ever find rest in community. I am tired, disillusioned. If it had been one church, two bad people, three rotten communities, I could have hung in there. I did.

But this last blow broke me, my Lord. I've looked in the face of an evil that can regard pure, unconditional love and grace and disdain them. There is brokenness, which is excusable, and then there is perversity— the incomprehensible evil. I now understand that unconditional love is irresistible to those with felt need, but it is abhorrent to those who have been inoculated against it.

Grace and sin abounded until neither felt relevant. Then redeeming love they took for granted, despite their refusal to admit a need for redemption.

So, what place have I among a people without need of redemption, grace, or mercy—a people without sin and in love with their own brokenness?

Father, I am a sinner, for I cannot do what you ask of me. I cannot love them. I have no love left to give. I can serve, but only as an empty shell and only for so long.

Forgive me, Lord. I *am* in need of grace and mercy—and redemption, if you have it.

PART ONE
Dependence

RECOLLECTION

With vinegar and honey
And whips and barbed hooks
And more stick than carrot
The world presents belonging
And brandishes it and attacks with it
The entrenchment and the fight
Drain the sunlight from my days
But in the dark, I find you waiting
Armed with basic acceptance
Then I am undone and refashioned
All in a moment, I am yours only
Every sunset is a prayer of recollection
Because your love is everything to me

VERTICAL RELATIONSHIP

There's no horizontal bar on my cross
Just one line running from you to me
Part of me wants to hope
Little buds will sprout outward into arms
But it must be enough for me
To sit here at your feet
And take shelter in your shade

GRACIOUS SOURCE

It doesn't take much
These days
For this little cup—
Read: 'thimble'—
To empty at the slightest
Tip
I find myself asking,
"Refill?"
Constantly
And you fill me

No one handles an "Up, please!"
Quite so graciously as you
My heart overflows with gratitude
That my form will never grow
Too heavy or too womanly
For your kind embrace
So, in gleeful jubilation, I may shout,
"Up, please!"

GOD OF MY CHILDHOOD, GOD OF MY WOMANHOOD

God of my childhood, God of my womanhood
You are the same yesterday, today, and forever
Though I fear myself from past to present to future
Your steadfast love casts out all fear
Holding time in your hands, you regard my lives
As one
And the strand that runs throughout
Is you

BETWEEN US

I have fasted intimacy for most of my life
The safe closeness of another body is a distant memory
If that
I wither and groan, dry and parched
I wish I had no need
I never wanted to want
You And
But here I am
So ashamed, at times, of this body
That wants so wantonly
It is between us
"But not in the way," you say

MY FRAME

You are the frame
On which my flesh hangs
Giving stability and structure
To this little blob
There's no mistake about it
It is on and in and through you
That I stand

SICKBED PRAYER

Kind Lover, you anticipate every need
My myopic mind cannot fathom
How wise, how good, how loving you are!
In sickness and in health, I revel
In the strength of your arms
And the steadiness of your grip
The sharpness of your ears
And the attentiveness of your gaze
Overwhelmed by life, I step back and lie down
To find Life in you

TETHER

You tether me to yourself
So the tides of time
Can't carry me off
Past and future clap together
And emotions foam and spray
I bob back and forth
But won't be swept away

MOMENT BY MOMENT

Moment by moment
I draw upon your strength
With every little breath
I breathe deeply of your grace
I need you
Love that steadies me
I need you
Truth to be my solid ground

MY ONE CONSTANT

Your friendship is my one constant
In all the changes of life
I try so hard not to need
But you expect that
And rejoice to be strong for me
To be present and available,
Attentive and kind for me
You are the God
Who sticks closer than any relative

RESPONSE

That you need, my love, is a given
But do not decide for me what is enough
You always accept little, trying not to take too much
Contentment is good, but don't settle
I say, my love, I will be extravagant with you
My little love who loves greatly and needs greatly
I will give you the desires of your heart
And I have loved you with an everlasting love

ETERNAL SAFETY

You are safe
Like the early hours of the morning
Before the world has gotten going
Before the troubles of the day come running
But you are timeless
And your safety extends throughout eternity

SECURE BASE

You are my secure base
So, while everyone else
Runs and screams
And chases and evades
I cling to you
Shyly toe-poking the dirt
And watching them

RIGHT FROM WRONG

Learning right from wrong
Is like learning to walk
I was used to standing on your feet
As you lifted me up at each step
Then you let me try on my own
And my fall felt very great
You dusted me off to try again

MUDDY SHOES

I present my heart to you
Like a toddler reveals her muddied shoes
Filthy and encrusted and waterlogged
Taking a single step can be perilous
Since mud-covered soles are slick
And walking is simply miserable
With all this yucky water in my socks
You could hear my approach from a mile back
Squishing and slipping and sobbing
I know I ought not to have walked there
In that place you told me to avoid
So, you don't belabor the point
Kindly, you clean me up,
Give me clean socks and fresh shoes
And with a little pat, you send me out again

HIDDEN GIFT

I wish you would lend me your perfection
So I could stand before the world
Repelling every criticism and complaint
But what you give is not so easily seen
From the outside, anyway
Your gift is what you take away
I sit before you alone
When I ask what you think
You answer with an embrace

OPEN TO ME

In a world with empathy like padded walls
I can't remember who locked me in
I wear self-respect like a straightjacket
To keep from casting pearls before swine
This takes everything into account
Except feelings, which intensify
And bruise without acknowledgement
Despite your vast awareness and responsibility
Your ears and heart are always open to me
And being heard sets this captive free

NEVER TO BE SOLD AGAIN

I am not at the mercy of anyone or anything
If I throw my whole self upon *your* mercy
Trauma lays its claim, along with the world's systems
But you bought me with your own self
Never to be sold again

THE ALONE MOMENT

You entreat me to open my eyes
And I see that the dark pit
In which I was buried
Was just the inside of my eyelids
Your light floods my being
And only the residue of that horror
The Alone Moment that shut my eyes
Remains as a sorrowful shadow
But that is all it is
When I'm with you
And you say you'll never leave
Even more, you say you were there

LOVE THAT SAVES ME

It is not the mere fact of love that saves me
But the presence of it that does
Your light piercing the darkness
Disrupting the reign of chaos
Your love giving me courage
To face that bad, mean pleasure
When it shows up, wild and fierce
And grabs me by parts I don't understand
To drag me back, back, back
To the bad, mean past
You are there—in the past
And here in the present, gentle and kind
To reveal that pleasure, in love, is safe
You are safe
And I, in you, am too

THE EDGE OF SELF-POSSESSION

You sit with me here on the edge of self-possession
Looking out over that chasm of hysteria
And I sometimes forget how far the fall could be
There are no guard rails here
But when I look at you, I'm unafraid
If I slip—which I sometimes do—
You pluck me right out of the air
And set me in your lap

STORY TIME

Demands, demands, demands
It's kind of comical
Like there was a stack of books
On a table near me
And someone grabbed the bottom one
Just for kicks
And now I'm on the floor
And the stack's a pile on top of me
But you're here, too
And you select a book
From the top of the pile
And read me a story
What would I do
Without story time?

YOU DO

I sometimes don't have enough love
To give, to receive, or to retain
In my little love reservoir for tough days
Does a source retain?
All I know is that
You *are* love
You have enough to give and to receive
And generously, you do
Delightedly, you do

REST

As I fall back on you
Everything comes into alignment
I am aware of aches and pains
That I powered through today
Your command, "Peace! Be still!"
Interrupted my busywork
Prying my grubby hands off
Of meaningless tools and tasks
That distract from pain
If only for a moment
Your invitation is not just to stop
But to rest, a practice and a skill
Which I still need you to teach me

A BREATH IN FOR GRACE

A breath in for grace
A breath out for love
I'm up in arms
I'm all worked up
A breath in for grace
A breath out for love
Emotions are a funny thing
Physiology is a bear
A breath in for grace
A breath out for love
Your aroma is most pleasant
Imparting life, even as I expire
A breath in for grace
A breath out for love

YOU MEET ME

You are solid truth
Unwavering as the world shifts
And melts around me
But you are also fluid
Flowing into all the hard-to-reach places
Where I've gotten stuck
And you meet me here

EVER-PRESENT

Your right hand leads me and holds me
If I say, "Surely, I am crushed under abandonment,"
Even the deepest recesses of my heart may be filled by you
Indeed, emptiness shall not hide from you
For, with you, the gaping chasm is brimming
Company and solitude are both alike to you

POWER TO TRY

I only exist when you see me
Thank you that your eyes will never depart from me
Other gazes accuse and banish
They impose
But yours embraces and emboldens
It calls to me
Saying, "Come forth, my love,
And remain."
With an audience of one, the One
I have power to try
Every moment of every day

BETTER THAN I COULD EVER

The peace that surpasses all understanding
Is a calm I cannot manufacture
When I'm ready to fight everyone and everything
Your refusal to be my adversary beckons
And when I come to you, you deescalate
Better than I could ever do it on my own
And when I am trapped in a flight pattern
Your still, small voice invites me
To stop fleeing in circles and come aside to rest
Better than I could ever do it on my own

YOU TAME ME

When the pain is too much
You ask to say hello to me
Astonishment is the correct response
To the fact that my maker
The King of the Universe,
Should request to greet his creation
But it is not the question that heals
Only the humbleness of your approach
And your willingness to interact
When I am wild
And you tame me

CRY DATE

I am a mess today
"My mess," you say
I am ugly and angry
I cannot be pleasant
And put together
And only-ever-agreeable
No, not today
But I am stuck
In my dutiful cheer
It is literally my job
So, you make a date
With me, to cry
Later today
Off-duty and safe
With you

DO NOT CALL ME NAOMI

When I wallow in speechless grief
You, in your exceeding goodness,
Give me words
To express valid but untrue feelings
So that we can relate in truth
Again

ENJOYMENT

Being with you is My Delight
If it felt nice and was empty
I would not enjoy it the way I do
My Delight is to enjoy you
Because you feel nice and you are nice
And more than that, you are kind
Which I've found, more and more,
Is not as low a bar as it seems

LOVE TO GO ON

You make me so happy, Lord
You are lovely and kind
And so very efficient
In two seconds or ten minutes
Or two hours or ten days
You manage to pour out
Just the amount of love I need
To go on

PART TWO
Cost

LOYALTIES CHANGE

Sometimes, I'm just bewildered
At how human loyalties change
Finding a path forward would be impossible
If I relied on their support
But you are the path
Though narrow, you are sturdy
Help my feet not to slip

People come and go
By nature, I guess
And loyalty flies away
Like leaves on the wind
Money can't buy it
Nor can winsomeness flow
Endlessly and without effort
But your friendship does
Without monetary value, but
At the cost of my throne
It is worth it

VINEYARDS

I look back on all the vineyards of my mother's sons
How much of myself I gave to tend their land!
Whether they kept all of the produce for themselves
Or torched the fields in which I toiled
My own vineyard wasted away from neglect
And I remain fruitless

YOUR PEOPLE

I am not the church by myself
But you are with me
And when I am among your people
I am the church along with them
No matter how they try to disown me

PINK DRESS

Your people try to squeeze the color out of me
With disparaging remarks and never-ending comparison
I dress only for you
And modestly to keep clear of stumbling block territory
But color is mine to enjoy
And a tasteful dress is cause to celebrate
They do not know how hard-won is my celebration
How, for years, I feared being a block to pastors
How, alone, I struggled to carry their sin
In my own body on my daily tree
Until your mercy intervened
So I could wear pink and hold my head high
So I could wear a dress and worship my God, my Love
In peace
They criticize what they do not know
And judge without understanding this healing
You have given me
Holy Love, they would not share my sorrow
And so, they cannot share my joy
Help me to celebrate this good work that you've started
That you will bring to completion in me

THIS LIFE WITH YOU

I guess I enacted transformational love incorrectly
Because I loved your people when they hated me
And they stayed hateful
I have turned my cheek so many times
I can't remember which was struck first
Throughout the generations, your people have destroyed
All that they knew to be holy
My Lord, I was willing to follow you
To join you in your death
But I lack the strength to live
This life with you

DISSOCIATED BODY

Lord, what will you do with your dissociated Body?
For the mind tries not to be embodied
And the members reject each other
Mistaking uniformity for unity and hating oneness
Who harmed your Bride so that she became
Like a woman using a mallet
To pound those lovely folds
Into which you've woven thousands of nerve endings?
She strikes and rips and punishes
Screaming that that one part should feel no pleasure
Since the whole has chosen not to
She would rather rip it out than receive
The gift you've given as a Husband to his Wife
Reveal the root cause of our trauma
And break that mallet in pieces
Help this little member, though unpresentable,
To function according to your good plan

CHURCH LAMENTATION

When everything I say and do
Can and will be used against me
You alone are my Judge and my Love
Help me to trust that
When the steadfast love of the church ceases
Your mercies won't ever come to an end
They are new every morning, yes, every morning
Great is your faithfulness, our Lord

WHY DO I NEED THE CHURCH?

I know why the church needs me
As with any institution
A younger, fresher presence is ideal
For survival's sake, if not for diversity of perspective

But why do I need the church?

Why do I need constant betrayal,
Backstabbing, backbiting, backwards
Gossiping slanderers and all those
Creeping, comparing oglers?

Why, I ask, do I need the church?

If I wanted an extra daily dose of poison
I would have stayed in high school
"Encouragement," they say
While dousing every living flame

FOR THE PKS

I don't understand
How a job can make
Hell invade Heaven
Community turn to isolation
And unity become division
You said you came to bring a sword
And turn children against their parents
But is this what you meant?

ABRAHAM'S FAITH

If Ishmael really Isaaced with Isaac
The way Isaac later Isaaced with his own wife
Then, Sarah was right to demand a separation
I still see how the situation could have been better handled
What I don't get is Abraham's next great idea:
Binding Isaac for sacrifice, reportedly at your command
But you can't have told him that!
Not you, rich in steadfast love
Not you, who plead the cause of widow and orphan
Not you, who gather your little ones under your wings

Abraham sent his firstborn to die in the wilderness
He then attempted to harm his secondborn
What was there to keep him from reanalyzing the situation
And all the jealousy, prejudice, and abuse in order to spiritualize
His newfound identity as "harmer of his children"?
What kept him from hearing his own guilt
And labeling it as your command?
What kept him from making his world whole again
By defining his faithfulness by his willingness
To harm his remaining child?

Good thing you are more faithful than Abraham
There was water in the desert and a ram in the bush
Abraham's faithfulness was in raising his eyes to look
His unintentional prophecy that prodded his son along
Was the foretelling of your merciful intervention
You commended Abraham's willingness to obey
Maybe because that moment of brokenness
In the father/son relationship was not the time to say,
"The cultures around you practice such things,
But I call you to be different."

YOU ARE GODS

I call it like I see it
David was a narcissistic tyrant
Who took what he wanted when he wanted
And stole and killed to maintain his power
Letting the vulnerable be ravaged
In his wake
And this, along with his songs, is his legacy

But before David was a tyrant
He was a shepherd in a field
A youngest brother hidden away
Doing a humble job in a humble time
And it seems few thought of him
One way or another
It was in this place that you chose him

But chose him for what?
To lead, yes; to shepherd, perhaps
But sheep-like people are worse than actual sheep
Because they are people
Shepherding them, you said, would be impossible
For any mere human
Because you knew the hearts of men

There is one called Good, who is a Shepherd
The rest are hired hands
My Lord, you warned us against our need
For one visible leader to rule and bind us
It is a felt need but not a true one
And in our false needs, we enact false worship
You said, "You are gods," but is this what you meant?

OUR OWN DEVICES

So, it was power that corrupted David
And Saul before him
And many priests and leaders, before and since
Mere men, most of whom sought your will—
But power, influence, and people's admiration
Are enough to ensnare any chosen one—
Men, chosen by God and by people
And what about those who come after them?
We are no less human, no less desirous
Of what only God should have

So, if people have not changed
Then, to what do you call us
As leaders of your people?
Surely not to be your competitors
As some state, not with their words
But certainly with their lives
Surely not to be graven images, created
In what we wish were our own likenesses
My God, don't call us if that's what we'll become
My God, don't leave us to our own devices

How far does your redemption reach?
Though you intended for it to go forth
From your heart through the church
(And perhaps it did, long ago)
We are too proud to acknowledge
Our need for it to double back on us
Grace and truth came through you
These are what we now need
Grace because sin abounds
And truth because we believe we have no sin

CHOSEN BY GOD

Call me an underminer and an interloper
But shouldn't parental instincts kick in
When a daughter lives in torment and without justice?
But men of God whose focus is the people of God
Place their children on the altar
Which is another way of saying, "washing their hands of it"
To be dismissed when calling attention to this
Would cause rage to rise in anyone
And convince them that a man after God's own heart
Is more likely coveting something rather than possessing it
It does make one wonder what it means to be chosen by God
And that those chosen by God are examples for the rest of us
Don't give me that "no one is perfect" bullshit
Indeed, no one is perfect, and people *will* make mistakes
But some let sin abound, believing that grace will abound
And those saddled with their sin learn
That grace and condemnation are one
If condemnation is the gospel
There is more than enough to go around
Like father, like son—
Because a daughter may be too downtrodden to try—
Two can play this game
And we will see on whom God's grace rests
We will see who is chosen by God

A PILLAR FOR ABSALOM

Absalom will always be a hero in my book
Not for his undermining of authority
Nor for his dashing good looks
Those he inherited from his father
Those and his use of sexual assault
As a tool to assert power

Absalom sought justice for Tamar, his sister
Ruthlessly, since she was denied it from above
What kind of father overlooks the assault of his daughter
Neglecting care of her and correction of her abuser?
A man chosen of God, I tell you
Years of power and favor will do that to anyone
Let the people suffer under David's power-drunk leadership
As they mistake anointing for irreproachability
But why must his daughter suffer—
And at the hands of another of her father's sons, no less?

Absalom was right to question
Though he was wrong to murder and rape
In his adoption of his father's methods
His campaign for justice disintegrated
It slipped like sand between his fingers
Like the years of life that he lost to rage
He had no sons to carry on his name
Just a daughter, his shattered sister's namesake,
So, he set up a pillar in the woods

Few men chosen of God will walk this broken road
In which a brother opens his heart to his sister's grief
And lives with her in the hell that is denial of justice
No wonder he undermined
No wonder he rampaged
No wonder he died

And God's chosen man continued his reign
David told Absalom's story in his own words
And lived to a gray old age
He is remembered well

But I remember God's unchosen
Not for the rock in the midst of the trees
But for the love that led him to his death
Hanging from a tree as he sought to set right
A grievous wrong done to his sister
Who, chosen or unchosen, was shattered

CHARISM OF THE UNCHOSEN

Some say they care, and maybe they do
Just not enough to stand up for what is right
Or to speak against what is wrong
Because, like the man of God,
The people of God are considered beyond criticism
Well, they are not beyond *my* criticism
It is the charism of the unchosen and the shattered
To call out the Lord's anointed
And I will. I will. I will.

THIS IS WHAT I HAVE TO SAY

Sweeping is actually men's work
When we're talking about survivors under the rug
But women sometimes too readily lift those woven corners
This is how beloved children of God respond to abuse of power
You all know what I'm talking about
I'm talking about that very transparent, humble man of God
The one you chose to mediate between you and your creator
And to be your redeemer and sustainer while he's at it
When it's your own fearless leader, do you ever face the truth
Or do you make yourself in his image
Doing as he says and does?
Worship yourself; worship him; it really doesn't matter
Either way, fear rules in the guise of complacency

YOUR SUFFERING SERVANTS

Beloved children, keepers of the peace, protectors of the anti-innocent
You've forced us to bear your griefs and your sorrows
While you label us "stricken by God"
But you are the ones who chastise us
To bring yourselves peace

Beloved children, deniers of humanity, punishers of the tormented
Many like sheep have gone astray
And turned, each one, to the same way
In which some have laid on others the iniquity of one and all
Hide your faces, despise us,
And see if any healing comes from these wounds

Beloved children, fig leaf weavers, holders of the dustpan and the rug
Oppress not and afflict not, and cover not our mouths
As we are cut off from our generation
Punished for our people's transgressions
So pleased are you to crush us and make us an offering for your sin

EXCUSES

Bathsheba wasn't David's only "mistake"
How long will you defend the man of God
With the shards of lives shattered
By his untempered lust and pride?
He excuses himself and calls it grace
Choosing to ignore that grace is no excuse
For abuse, and he will stand before God
On that quavering mound of chaff

SON OF DAVID

Son of David, have mercy on me
Because I am silenced and no one takes up my cause
Son of David, have mercy on me
Because I have no more strength to remain silent
Son of David, have mercy on me
Because I reject the anointing of predators
Son of David, have mercy on me
Because I long to make my tormentors pay

For whom have I come searching
And who will answer me?
Though I am born from above
I also have been born from within
One feels like waiting for a parent
Who keeps looking the other way
The other is a compulsion to take action
But using the methods of wrongdoers
So, I do not know whose name I call
When I call upon the Son of David

RESPONSE

I weep with you, my love
And I understand your anger and your pain
May I touch them?
May I sit with you in your grief?
May I take the Davids from your hands
And the Absaloms from your heart?
Tears are okay, and questions even more so
I will be Brother and Father to you
Standing with you in loyal solidarity
While, from my throne, orchestrating
The redemption of all things
Until then, this shall be your pillar:
Hope

SAME GOD

My God, you do things that I wish you wouldn't
And you allow to happen things that break my heart
But others in your church worship a God who blesses
Everything they do
Whenever they decide to act in hate
Or write a manifesto to which they may affix your name
Their God's head waggles in delight
Tell me what I've missed here
Because following you has cost me everything
But they claim to follow you without loss
And, in fact, take from those who have nothing
Is it possible that we are all seeking the same God
But we end up worshipping vastly different ones?

WHAT ABOUT *ME*?

Help me to see how I was merely pressed
And not entirely crushed
I know you never abandoned me

I picked up my cross daily
But started to wonder if daily death
Included daily resurrection

What about *me*?
Was it hard for you to emerge from the tomb, or did you
Walk with no limp because your wounds were blessèd ones?

I am stuck between death and resurrection
Knowing that getting up faithfully can only lead to death again
On this side of eternity

What about *me*?

NOTHING LEFT TO GIVE

You said I cannot love my God and hate my brother
So, I do not love you
My loving God, my Pearl of Great Price
I've sold all I had
To have and to hold you
For richer, for poorer, for better and for worse
But Sweetness of All Sweetness, Star That Lights My Days,
I do not love you, not for lack of will
But for lack of strength
For from where shall love spring
When my heart has been torn out?

God be merciful to me, a sinner
I cannot love your people
As you have loved me: boundlessly
I am small and finite
When I am wounded, I die
In three days, I rise again with scars
But I neither walk through walls nor ascend
To sit at the right hand of God the Father Almighty
Forgive me
For the church is not the joy set before me
As we were before you
What I do is not for them
I denied myself, took up my cross every day
And now there is nothing left to give

PRE-CREATIVE CHAOS

Sometimes we find ourselves in the heart of Babylon
And that's okay
I mean, it's not
But what can we do?
Was it that your city was invaded
Or that its rulers hired destroyers
To do the work for which they had no stomach?
Or did they announce brazenly their intention
And stand between you and your people
Taking advantage of humanity's attraction
To all things apprehensible to the five senses?

No answer is satisfactory
So, at the end of the day
As we acknowledge how Babylon and the Holy City
Sometimes seem indistinguishable
And exile and residing in one's own land
Have become one and the same
We must rejoice!
For dividing walls of moral high ground brought down
Level us into unity
How great is our need!
How utterly weak we are!
And over amorphous chaos, your Spirit hovers
On the cusp of an extraordinary creative act

WITHOUT RESERVATION

You forgive me without reservation
I confess, you absolve, and it is gone
Teach me to be like this
Help me to be like this
I know it is not an action
It is a way of being
Your being
You, the one I want and need
I'm believing
Like love, all-believing
Faith, with hope, in action
Help me to be like this
Teach me to be like this
To confess, to absolve, and see it gone
To forgive all without reservation

THE DENIERS

It is easier to forget than to forgive
Not the acts, but the people
How easily I push them to the corners of my mind
They who denied me human dignity
I shall deny their existence
I am pleased to forget because
I make them go away
If they don't exist, maybe the wound won't either
If only

Everything remembers; this place, these things,
My body, my soul, just not my mind
I carry these deniers in me
And stuff denial like lint in the wound
I cannot forget because
I view the world through them
Captive to words acted out, but
Never spoken, blinders
Unholy

MAKER

Betrayal is a bitter friend
That makes aborted friendship
Preferable
Deception kills intimacy
So, maybe I didn't end this
I don't know how to make things right
An "I forgive you" meaningfully uttered
Doesn't make a liar trustworthy
Nor does it cause a rebel to repent
So, my job is not to *make* a person
Anything
In fact, I may ask forgiveness of the Maker
For ascribing identities to the Creation
Forgive me. I do not understand
What I have called out of a broken vessel
I do not know what I have perpetuated in this
Naming
I cannot make things right
You are the one who makes
You make things
And you make them right
Forgive me, for I know not what I do

WHEN I THINK OF THE CHURCH

When I think of the church
First, I think of promise
Your promise to make us like you
And to love the world with and through us
Second, I think of cruelty
Your people's propensity for it
And how it spews outward and inward
Certainly, we have dug a deep pit
And fallen into it ourselves

But there are these small seeds of kindness
One act by a sister or brother, here or there
Short moments of camaraderie and mercy
Nestled in the substance of my heart
Far beneath the claw marks of my greatest fans
You somehow nurture these tender heart sprouts
And in your kindness, they remain in me
And I in you

YOU'RE DIFFERENT

Grace and ecstasy
Being one with you
Sheds pretense in a moment
Blinding light made visible
Pure, cleansing
Unapproachable, inviting
All-holy, enfolding
This confused and ragged heart
You gently dab at condemnation's wounds
"I'm different," you say.
And I believe you

YOU DO IT BETTER

You do it better, Sacrificial Love
But you still praise
My blotchy, half-destroyed canvas
As a great masterpiece
You lift my head to see
A mosaic of mosaics, and I do see
The greatest masterpiece

PART THREE
Faith

BROKEN FAITH

"Faith is trust," they say
So, with broken trust comes broken faith
I cannot power through this one
The best I've got is devotion
That I love you and must stay with you
Because we are so intertwined
I cannot live without you
And so, if there is any trust
It is only in this:
Our definitions of "good" differ
I don't like it, but what can I do?
Leave?
You are my life

PREVENIENT LOVE

I love you because you first loved me
And that prevenient love I do trust
I do not understand its mechanics
I do not understand the finer points
Like why you allow tragedy
And how I can ask you for help
And feel as though you have refused
But that your love holds all things together
And in your loving being all things consist
I do trust
You are faithful
In this I do trust

ONLY TO YOUR WILL

The story of the greatest person
From among those born of women
Ascends through strength of spirit,
Conviction, boldness, and influence
Only to decline sharply and end most abruptly
Pointlessly, it seems, at least in this life

The least in the kingdom is greater than he
Am I the least or somewhere in the unhappy middle?

When lust, vindictiveness, and greed
Flex their ill-gotten power
Give me the strength to kneel
Before a taker of life
While remaining subject
Only to your will

DIRECT MY EYES

Give me what I need
To stand within a ruined city
Watching for the enduring one to come
Stop my tortured ears
To the voices of those who set fire
To the life's work I thought you'd blessed
When the symbol of your promise
Reduces to ashes and scatters
Under the derisive feet of haters
Direct my eyes

I AM NOT FAITHFUL

I am not faithful; I am angry
My confessions of truth are drowned in bitter tears
Right action is an empty shell
My desires cannot align with yours
Because I have only one desire:
For the pain to stop

I BOUGHT A PEARL

I sold all that I had and bought a pearl
At least the guy that bought the field
Had treasure to keep or sell
And his own lot on which to build
A place to live, but I have a pearl
Which I must keep and cannot sell
And my, it is a beautiful pearl!

THORNY

Forgive my thorny soil, Lord
And if you are willing
Remove these thorns
How can my soil be good
When I can't catch a break?

GIVE ME FAITH

Give me faith
To see my desires fade
While believing your answer
Will be better than I ever
Could have dreamed

DON'T PUT ME OUT

Forgive me, Lord
For ridiculing you
When you say
The girl is only sleeping
Don't put me out
With the crowd
Let me stay and see
What I never believed
To be possible

TIGHTROPE

I don't know how to walk the tightrope
Of "my God will rescue me, but even if God doesn't…"
And I hope the chasm across which it stretches
Is not unfaithfulness

YES AND AMEN

All the promises, in you, are Yes
And, in you, Amen
But what, actually, have you promised?
Not to leave me; that I know
But everything else is distant,
Nebulous, and maybe just promised
To someone else, somewhere else
And I am left with the question
Of whether your presence is sufficient
The right answer is Yes
Help me to feel it
Amen

WAITING ON THE WATER

Now would be a good time
For you to come, walking on the water
The wind has been against me
And I've been rowing all night
I stepped out a few times
Believing I could walk on the water
But now that I'm cold, stiff,
And nearly half-drowned
I really hope that when I receive you
Into my boat
We'll arrive at our destination
Immediately

BOTTOM-FEEDER

Perhaps it wasn't faith
When I could see the end
I didn't mean to trust
In my ability to hold on
But now, show me faith
When all directions are confused
Except for up and down, and I am sinking
Down to where light can't reach
I've become a bottom-feeder
Dwelling in obscurity and feeding on rot
Does "faith in" include "faith that"
And if "that", then what?

I HATE DESTINY

I hate destiny
And all words appealing to my desire for purpose
But destiny is the worst
Because it makes it sound faithful
To take my eyes off of you
To scan the horizon
For some vehicle by which
You'll pick me up from the miry clay
Setting my feet on a rock
I then believe will catapult me
To my greatest potential and self-defined fulfillment
Missing entirely that my end and completion
Are only in you, my Rock and Redeemer
My faithful friend
Deliver me from tickled ears and a fickle heart
And have mercy on these, your people,
So mistaken as to claim destiny
As gospel

FAITH OBSTACLE

My Lord and Love
Don't let my faith stand
At the expense of our relationship
That I'd believe your words as fact
Only to cut off my heart
From the very Love that is my source

DEFINING FAITH

You are not confined
To the limits of mere humanity
Exhausted and sleep-deprived
So, why now do you feign slumber
In the bow of the boat
While the storm rages
And waves overwhelm me?
I call to you, and you don't hear
Or, I fear, you won't hear
Show me whether faith is
Waiting until you decide to act
With one command, stilling the storm
Or whether faith is shouting at you
Until you stop ignoring me

FISTS

When words fade
All I have are fists
The white-knuckled kind
That babies use to cling
To their mother's shirt
And when fists fail
There are your arms
Secure, unworried, caring

FAITH LIKE CUDDLING

Sometimes faith is like cuddling
In the absence of words
Presence and attention are enough
I belong to you and you to me

RESPONSE

"You trust with the little faith you have," you say,
"And it is enough."
This, too, is faith
That I trust our bond
That you have come to live in me
And you won't leave
Because you said you wouldn't

SURRENDER

To entrust myself to you
Surrendering my resources and relationships
My existence
I return to that first bestowal of life
Knowing that you can take or add
As much as you please
It was never really mine
To keep

THE MESSENGER

Sometimes you lend us faith
By pouring it like water
Into parched and aching souls
Other times you lend faith
By sending a messenger
Weathered and tested
And having withstood
To attest that the Omega
Is the same as the Alpha, and
Although mere humans do not end
Where we begin
You are constant

I DON'T WANT TO ASK

It astounds me that you ask me to ask you
When you've denied my most ardent requests
Time after time after time
I don't *want* to ask you
But the softness of your heart
Beckons to me and softens mine
And I don't know what to do

PAINFUL PRAYER

I know my prayers don't fall on deaf ears
But sometimes it would be easier to believe they did
Because it hurts to know that you hear my frantic cries
And then make me wait for deliverance

PRAYER BATTLE

Why do I battle in prayer
When the battle belongs to you?
Why do I ask you for anything?
I did not want to say
I don't think you listen
When I cry to you for a good cause
On this side of heartbreaking nos,
I now regard with perplexity
The times you said yes

THE LINE

I don't know where the line is
Between faith and resignation
I believe you *can* help me
I don't know if you *will*
And if you don't, you're still good
I waited for so long
Hearing my own desires
Rather than your voice
Now I trust nothing I hear
And I wait
Because either you'll help me
Or you won't, and you're still good

I MISS YOU, SWEET LOVER

I miss you, Sweet Lover
I'm mad at you, and I love you
And I don't want you at arm's length
I'm mad at you, and be near me
I am in need of you
I miss you, Sweet Lover
I love your voice and your touch
More than my own vindication
I love you
More than the supposed love of people
I miss you, Sweet Lover
Come be near me, I pray
If I must release my life's desires
I beg you, don't release me
Forgive my turning in despair
I miss you, Sweet Lover

FAITHFULNESS ENOUGH

The peace that surpasses all understanding
Is that you are, and you are with me
Where intellectual navigation fails
I am anchored in your steadfast love
Nothing unsettles you; you've seen it all before
Here, with you, I am accepted
In my doubt and fear and rage
And in your heart, I find faithfulness
Enough for both of us

PARALYTIC WITH NO FRIENDS

If I am a paralytic with no friends
Jesus, be my friend
Carry me to the roof
And lower me to yourself
By *your* faith, forgive my sins
By *your* faith, make me well
I know that you are willing

GIFT OF FAITH

Strange
That faith is what I need
To be faithful to you
But my finite self cannot produce
Perfect or even endless faith
To pursue and catch hold of you
So, you lend me yours
Like giving a child money to practice
Buying groceries or counting change
For what do you train me?
Or maybe it is not training but charity
You know that my need is great
Greater than I can afford
In a transactional arrangement
So you give, so I can have something
To give back to you
So you give to me and give

About the Author

Naomi M. Wong is a Black and Chinese author of religious poetry and speculative fiction. This is her third book of poetry and her fifth book, in total.

Also by Naomi M. Wong

POETRY

My Delight in My Beloved: A Single Woman's Song of Songs

Healing Beauty

EVOLUTION OF CONTROL SERIES

Amphibious

Bivalent

www.ingramcontent.com/pod-product-compliance
Lightning Source LLC
Chambersburg PA
CBHW030556080526
44585CB00012B/395